On Depression

On Depression

Belle H. Justiniani

RESOURCE *Publications* • Eugene, Oregon

ON DEPRESSION

Copyright © 2021 Belle H. Justiniani. All rights reserved. Except for brief quotations in critical publications or reviews, no part of this book may be reproduced in any manner without prior written permission from the publisher. Write: Permissions, Wipf and Stock Publishers, 199 W. 8th Ave., Suite 3, Eugene, OR 97401.

Resource Publications
An Imprint of Wipf and Stock Publishers
199 W. 8th Ave., Suite 3
Eugene, OR 97401

www.wipfandstock.com

PAPERBACK ISBN: 978-1-6667-3055-5
HARDCOVER ISBN: 978-1-6667-2222-2
EBOOK ISBN: 978-1-6667-2223-9

SEPTEMBER 27, 2021

Contents

Preface | vii
Disclaimer | ix
Acknowledgments | xi

On Depression

Darkness | 1
Evening Musings | 3
Riots | 5
Untitled | 6
28 | 8
The Hardest Poem I'll Ever Write | 10
Depression | 14
An Ode to Dysthymia | 19
Facts (Anatomy of a Sleepless Night) | 23
Fire | 25
Boredom | 28
Sensory Overload | 30
Rut | 31
In the Rain | 34
Metaphors | 37
Stairwell | 39

Better Times | 41
A Little Hint of Hoping | 43
Muse | 46
Mocha | 49
Whiskey | 50
Lucky, Pt. 1 | 53
Lucky, Pt. 2 | 56
An Open Letter to My Heart | 59
Soulmate | 62
Clapback | 65
The Body I Bear | 69
Youth, Pt. 1 | 72
Youth, Pt. 2 | 74

Preface

I'VE BEEN WRITING POEMS SINCE I was a child, long before I knew what depression was. When I was diagnosed with Major Depressive Disorder in my early twenties, poetry quickly became an outlet for me to express myself.

And then, a few years later, I heard about a schoolmate who had committed suicide. Before he died, he'd written an open letter talking about his own experience with depression. The letter circulated and eventually made its way to me. When I read it, I was filled with immense sadness and, at the same time, great awe at how he'd described the condition. Never before had I felt so heard, and it was by someone who had never even met me. It was at that moment that I vowed to do what he'd done before he passed—be a voice for the voiceless, for those whose voices have been shattered by despair. And, if I was lucky, maybe giving them a voice would also give them hope.

To the few people I shared my poems with, I was presenting an inside look at both the darkest and most hopeful recesses of my mind . . . to my readers now, I offer the knowledge that you are not alone, that I am praying for you, and that if you lack the words, you can borrow mine.

Disclaimer

I HAVE TO WARN YOU before you step into my written world: this is not a happy book. I don't delve into physical self-harm because I've never felt the urge for it, but emotional self-harm is something I am very familiar with, as are many people with depression. I should also warn you that if you are in a dark place in your life and are having doubts of whether this might trigger you, it's probably better not to read this book. But if you can make it to the end, I promise you that there is hope . . . both at the literal end of this book, and in your metaphorical tunnel.

I should also inform you: this is not a sad book either. Depression aside, I have always been the bearer of a pesky sense of hope. I won't sugarcoat every poem with a cheesy little speech, but I can't stay true to myself without admitting that I have fortunately managed to find hope in even the darkest places. Sometimes that reflects in my poems; sometimes it doesn't.

Like I said, this collection details my innermost thoughts from both the hardest and happiest times of my life, interspersed with narratives of my experiences for context. I hope that in some way it eases your pain, whether by giving you a voice, showing that you are not alone, or aiding your recovery somehow.

Wherever you are and however you ended up with this book, know that I believe in you, and will always be hoping for a happier future for all of us.

There is something to be said
About the power of poetry
It's nice to know the words within my head
Can impact you, and not just me

If you listen close you'll hear my tale
Of depression and its aftermath
If you pay attention then you wouldn't fail
To know how I carved my path

If you're like me, then I don't mind
If you'd like to borrow these words
Use them till you're satisfied
And invite others to our world

And if you're not, then welcome, too
If you'll allow me to take your mind for a spin
You might gain something that helps you
Understand this crazy world you're in

Whoever you are, you're welcome here
And thanks for hearing me out
I'll take the wheel if you'll allow me to steer
Your journey with me begins now

Acknowledgments

Thank you to my parents—my constants and confidants, my sanctuary and lighthouse.

Thank you to my brother—my inspiration and example in more ways than one.

Thank you to my extended family—my fairy godmothers, my council of elders, and my girls.

Thank you to the lovely people at Wipf and Stock, who helped me bring this dream to life.

Thank you to my cover editor, who took charge of my book's first impression.

Thank you to my friends, who blew up group chats and video calls when I announced my book.

Thank you to my therapists, who were pivotal in my road to recovery.

Thank you to my support groups, who inspire me every single day.

And thank you most of all to God, who put just the right amount of roadblocks and victories on my path to happiness.

Darkness

Depression has been described to me in a number of ways: a hormonal imbalance, a persistent feeling of despair, a clawing shadow trying to block out all the light. I've always thought of it in the context of darkness—something that deadens your senses and makes you feel instinctively afraid.

Trigger-happy
Darkness
Always within reach
It bends
To every thought
Lies in waiting

It makes a fool
Of simple joys
It mocks control
And flashes its smile
Exploding
Behind closed eyelids

Darkness slips
A snake constricting
Lungs collapse
And eyes fall shut
The heart pounds like love
But oh, this isn't love

Brick after brick
We built more
Than just walls

The worst part
Is the ceiling
That keeps out the light

Say hello to
The darkness
That lives in your heart

Evening Musings

Back in college, I lived in a dorm. My nights walking to the dorm were often the quietest, easiest times to contemplate. Around the time my depression kicked in, they also became the times my sadness would demand to be acknowledged. On one such night, I decided to put it all into words.

One day I woke up
And I didn't have dreams anymore

One day I woke up
And the sun forgot to rise

One day I woke up
And there was a weight on my back

It didn't lighten
And neither did I

One night I went home
And the road was darker than it had ever been

One night I went home
And the sky felt too quiet

One night I went home
To find that home was gone

What difference one day makes
And things do change overnight

Each day I wake up
And each night I go home

And I ask the world if things will change
I know they will, because the days go on
And nights keep chasing after them

What no one sees when they say the dawn follows night
Is that each day always ends
And that some people make their own darkness

Riots

This poem, like "Darkness," was written at a time when the smallest things would trigger my worst symptoms. In this instance, the trigger was a negative comment I read online—not about myself, but about a celebrity I followed. When the sadness became too much, I decided to write. That eased the pain a little.
The smallest things can have the biggest impacts. Please be kind when you post.

My brain riots
Trigger words start the dance
Riots
I never stood a chance
And I
Don't know what's going on in the other half of the world
But solidarity and compassion
Only make the riots start
And they tear apart my insides
And the world begins to spin
And the riots keep on going
Need to let the demons in
Let them dance their little party
Let them break apart the throne
Let them tear at every muscle
Let them scratch at every bone
And the sound, it always rises
Higher and higher until
There's nothing left
And I'm here
As my brain riots

Untitled

I wish someone had told me
That there would come a day
When nothing would be good enough

And the joy would be so far,
Half a universe away
And the words would fail

What do you do
After the tears have been cried?
How do you move when you're stationary?

Where do you go
When home isn't here?
What more can you say?

When the ache feels implosive
And yet eyes are dry,
What happens next?

What more can you do
In this dead-end world?
Your hands shake when you're fragile

Do you shatter some more
When you're made of broken shards?
What does it take to fall apart?

How much strength does it take
To say goodbye permanently?
Or is it cowardice?

I don't need silence
I also don't need words
What comes next when you're broken, anyway?

I want to move
And I want to stay
Most of all I just want to sleep

And the tears don't fall
Because what good would that be?
Rock to the mirror, keep shattering me

Is it all in my head?
Am I just sensitive?
The worst part of all this is it's all because of me

I wish it was all as easy
As definition, poetry
But when is anything ever simple?

From cracks to shatters
From crystals to dust
Don't put me back together; there's nothing to see

Turn away before you can't
I'm not on display
Run before it's too late

It's so hard to cover up
Volatility
But the emptiness remains in me

28

I don't think I'll ever be ready
To say these words to you
I don't even know
If I can put pen to paper
And write out the truth
How you scare me like you do
And how it hurts to love you so

When I think of you, it's sadness
At the forefront of my mind
It's hopelessness and sorrow
And dreams left to die in the dark
And it's hard to really think of you
Because I don't want to see that pain

I can't honestly describe you
Because "trapped" is what comes to mind
And various other broken things
It's so hard to pretend
That we're not torn up about all this

I wish there was something I could do
But the truth is that there isn't
Maybe that's the lesson here:
To accept what can't be changed

But is it wrong for me to hope?
Sometimes it hurts just to try
Ironic to think I'm more hopeless than you

Don't mistake this for condemnation
I'm just airing out my truth

It doesn't change how I feel about you

The Hardest Poem I'll Ever Write

I'll confess: I've always been a sucker for fame. I wanted to be many things—an award-winning author, a renowned singer, a polished actress, a secret celebrity. Anything, really, as long as it meant fame and fortune.

Was I after the money? No. I think the appeal was in being loved by so many.

Has that dream changed? I certainly hope so. I'd like to think I'm here for more than just to make myself happy.

On a lonely night in April
I sat and found my truth
As tears ran freely down my cheeks
And my mind no one could soothe

And I tried putting it in words,
The code that I've lived by
I don't think I'll do it justice
But, by God, I guess I'll try

I'm a girl who dreams of being adored
And lives in fantasy,
Who hasn't learned yet to grow up
And in fame finds ecstasy

I'm a girl who refuses to chase her dream
Because to try means learning to fail
Refusing to pull my own anchor up
So my ship will never sail

I'm a girl whose mind keeps running
Longing for one thing, holding back
I think I'm meant for bigger
But I'll always go off track

It's not just about laziness
There's more to it than that
(At least I really hope it's so
And I'm not just some brat)

1.

Things have always gone well for me
Without work on my part
So much so that I don't know
How to put passion into art

2.

I've failed before and subsequently
Felt the world come crashing down
I never knew how to forgive myself
Or turn my pride around

3.

My mind finds dead ends everywhere
My sickness wills it so
So what's the point in going on,
If the end I already know?

4.

I'm scared of failure and success
I'm scared they'll feel the same
I'm scared my whole life's work will be
Just Someone else's game

5.

I don't know if it's meant for me
I won't know till I'm gone
I will my body to try anyway
But my limbs, they weigh a ton

Are all these just excuses?
To my ears they seem to be
But even as I read them through
There's truth in what I see

So maybe my real truth is
That I'm a coward and a fraud
I put up a face of confidence
But inside I'm distraught

I pretend to have it all on track
I act like I'm okay
But deep inside I know my truth:
I dread every single day

And I won't make false promises
Of how I know it'll get better than this
Because I don't see truth in that
It's not real to me like this is

I wish I could stop dreaming
Of a life beyond my own
Or I wish it were handed right to me
Or developed as I'd grown

But that's not how life works
And death may not be better
I don't really know what more to say
I've said it to the letter

I'd pray or cry or talk it out
But what good would that be?
Without my truth out in the air,
Could anyone help me?

So here it is, old universe
My truth for all to see
I bare my soul because I'm through
Make what you will of me

Depression

How do I begin
To discuss what the problem is?
Where do I start
When the sky is cloudy gray?

How do I say
What I never had words to describe?
And what do I do
When this is the life I've been living?

I can't say what's wrong with me
I can't say where it began
There are no words that tell the story

There's a weight on my chest
Like a lie that pulls me down
And never seems to ease

Addicted to the pity
Or addicted to the pain
Why are you like this?

Scared of being lonely
Or scared of being home
Scared most of all of feeling
Like neither really exists

Am I just being selfish,
Or is there more to who I am?
They said I had a good heart
And I had to struggle to believe it was true

I don't know what I wish for
I want to want again
I want to believe in tomorrow

Is this still the sickness
Or is this who I am?
Where does it end; where do I begin?

I crave and I cry
I leap and I weep
I am a manic episode

I am every conundrum
I'm a tightrope walker
I'm a storm inside a bottle
I am everything and nothing at once

But I am tired and I'm weary
I have nothing left to give
I've never been so hollow
And the future has never felt so hopeless before

I moan and I mumble
I lose sight of all my dreams
My words jumble both inside and out

Why does it hurt you?
Why wish you could feel sad again?
And why can't you have it?

Indistinct mutters
Are shouts in reality
Much like the voices in my head

My chest constricts
And pain clouds my mind
How do I describe these feelings?
Do I call them "it" or do I call them "me"?

Was there ever a me beyond it?
If it's been around for so long
It's as much a part of me as I've ever known
What am I giving up by giving it away?

I want to scream and I want silence
I want the world to stop
But I'll settle for sleeping

Tomorrow it restarts
I know that for sure
But nothing changes and nothing's new

Maybe tomorrow the tears can fall
And even though it'll never be enough
It'll be enough

If I tell no one
Will that make it any less real?
If I put a smile on once a day
They'll believe me

I won't, but I don't matter
Perception is all that does
Because pain is a friend I've had
For too long to leave behind

It hurts to imagine
It hurts even more to think
My nightmare and daydream are one and the same

Cry tonight, or be a shell
It's a simple question
With a consistent answer

Show me love that matters
Show me how to love myself
I need proof that love exists

I need security and comfort
I breed jealousy and hurt
Something needs to stop
But what am I to do?

Let me go but keep me here
Say goodbye but never leave
If opposites attract
No wonder I'm self-absorbed

Hug the pain away, or try to
Kiss the wound to make it bleed
Let me go under

The water has never felt so calm
Bliss that ebbs and flows
Let me sink like a stone

One night of sanity
Bears three weeks of joy
I'd take the pain over the pleasure

There's a silence in my head
So loud it's worse than screams
I want to cry
But there are no tears behind my eyes

Calm the storm
Pull the waves back from the shore
Make the echoes stop
Tell the choirs to stop singing

The bad thing about going on
Despite the everyday pain
Is never knowing it's not all in your head

Leave me alone
Leave me alone
Leave me alone

Stay with me
I don't even know
Who I'm talking to anymore

An Ode to Dysthymia

Dysthymia, or Persistent Depressive Disorder, is a condition characterized by depressive symptoms occurring for a long time—for example, from adolescence to adulthood. It's not as intense as Major Depressive Disorder, but from what I understand, it lasts longer and is more constant throughout one's daily life.
Back when we were wondering if dysthymia was my condition, my psychologist described it as "a sadness that weaves through life." A few days after she told me that, I wrote this poem.

They ask me how I'm doing
And what answer can I give?
Don't they understand I'm grieving
'Cause that's the only way I know how to live

I've learned to stop asking
How I can be happy when I'm sad
At the very least it's something
That I can sometimes say I'm glad

I lose myself in senses
In tastes and smells and sounds
I've lost all my defenses
And the world that spins around

Is a cruel world, I know
And I've learned to live with that
I've learned to let things go
And take the good times with the bad

So marginally it's better
Though I fear it'll never change
Does my mood shift with the weather?
Or will it always be this strange?

Will the darkness overtake me,
Or will the light come through?
Or will neither outcome prove to be
The only thing that's true?

Will it be this way forever?
And will I always feel so lost?
Am I not destined for better?
And if so, then at what cost?

I've learned to function through the pain
Of that, I'm proud to say
But is that all there is to gain?
'Cause that's my everyday

Is everyone around me
Feeling this way, too?
Are all our glasses empty?
And is the world so blue?

Oh, dysthymia, so poetic
"A sadness that weaves through life"
Neither manic nor cathartic
Just an ever-present strife

And the thing about this madness
Is that it all seems so mundane
Do we all have that sadness?
Is that what makes us the same?

Is all that I've been facing
Just a part of humankind?
Am I just overreacting,
Is it all a trick of the mind?

Do I even have a sickness?
Or is the world too much for me?
Is there an end to this, my weakness?
Is there an escape from melancholy?

I live with base distractions
My phone is my best friend
And all these small attractions
Well, never will they end

Because the world, it keeps on turning
And each morning I awake
And face the day that's coming
For my friends' and family's sake

While inside I am empty
A little happy, a little sad
A whole lot melancholic
But I guess I'm okay with that

Because alternatives aren't better
And I would never ask for worse
It's bittersweet to the letter
When roaring fire turns to embers

I used to be passionate
I used to love true
Now I don't know who I like or hate
And my interactions, they are few

Oh, dysthymia, you're a killer
A thief of hopes and dreams
You're silent and you're bitter
You're much more than you seem

And sometimes I'm so angry
On times I let you in
But you're cruel and you're petty
Just you watch; I won't let you win

I know it's you that makes me think
I'm stuck like this forever
You throw me in and watch me sink
But trust me, I know better

And I won't lose out to you
I'll plant a newer seed
Things will change, I'll believe that's true
And improve, they will indeed

Facts (Anatomy of a Sleepless Night)

On my loneliest nights I snuff out my own spark
Contemplate on life and give in to the dark
Swallow bitter pills that seem to have no end
And think of the facts that are hard to contend:

The people we love make it so hard to love them
Anger and sadness, they oft work in tandem
Sometimes no words can explain how we feel
The best kind of world is one that isn't real

The world's got predators on the attack
And you're powerless in a night so black
The people who matter don't always stay
And hurt will never really go away

In all that it's hard to get up and move on
You can't see a thing when clouds block the sun
You can't move a muscle when there's nowhere to go
You can't feel authentic when it's all for show

My breathing gets shallow while my stare runs deep
Like rivers my eyes run and I cannot sleep
And when it's all over and my cheeks have dried,
There's a lonely soul left when the tears have been cried

And finally after all that release
I find myself calmer yet more ill at ease
And more often than not I just drift away
Let time take care of what happens the next day

But other times, I lie awake
Caught in between what's real and what's fake
And find myself unable to deny
That I can see kinder facts if I only try

For example, the fact that I can see
My reflection when my cat stares at me
Or that I still dance when certain songs play
And there are still affirmations left for me to say

My favorite color's that of the clothes I wear
And I love the smell of my newly-washed hair
I sink into pillows and cuddle in sheets
Dreaming of places and people to meet

And the people I love, though flawed they may be
They've all contributed to me being me
And while my spark is snuffed out tonight
Each morning brings with it a new flame to light

And all of these facts, they may seem so small
So insignificant in the face of it all
But while that may be true, it's still nice to find
Their comforting swell in the recess of my mind

And I tell myself that maybe that's all it takes
To keep going through the struggle that every day makes:
A reminder to myself that some facts provide ease
And familiarizing myself with facts such as these

Fire

"Fire" is about confidence. I've always been called confident, but it wasn't until I wrote this poem that I realized how beguiling false confidence can be. It was also when I wrote this poem that I learned of a different kind of confidence—the kind that comes with true acceptance of who you are, faults and all.

Do I have to kill my fire
Just to keep myself alive?
Do I give up the best part of me
So that everything else can survive?

I'm a thread that is still fraying
I'm a birdsong unsung
I've a heart that is still trying
To carve out of a bruised lung

And find its home somewhere
On a world without me
I've a mind that is still living
By the need to stay free

Without knowing that somewhere
Deep in my cold, dark soul
My freedom is a prison
My fire is a role

A role I have played
Once so very well
But I've found is now shattering
Just another brittle shell

Because what I've long been hiding
In a corner tucked away
Is a heart that burns brighter
Than the strongest light of day

And maybe for the first time
I can put trust in that flame
And maybe, just maybe
My life will never be the same

Because this new flame I'm carrying
It's stronger than I was
And the new me is strong enough
To break my old cage of glass

A cage I hadn't thought of
A cell I hadn't seen
Made of fear at what comes after
And rage at what had been

What once I thought was fire
I now see for what it's worth:
A door I could only see through
That prevented my rebirth

Because the fire I kept so dearly
All this time has held me back
And the flame that I now carry
Has me on a better track

To finding my voice and getting my peace
To raising my sword and proclaiming me
To letting my light be a beacon to all
To being myself, and being free . . .

Finally.

Boredom

This and the next few poems tackle a specific symptom of depression that I feel quite often—a lack of motivation. You'd be surprised how strongly I feel about being bored.

Set me on fire
Give me something to live for
Cast me in iron
Give me someone I can love

Take this boredom
And set it aflame
Show me something I can enjoy

Because everything is fleeting
Smiles are few and far between
Blank looks and stares on paper

Would that something happens
Would that time moves on
Would that my brain feels
Less like a rolling mess
In a body frozen in time

Would that songs have meaning
And words don't lose their luster
And eyes don't lose their shine

Nervous tics take over
As my gaze flits place to place
My mouth fills with bile
Yet I sit here motionless

Frozen, ever frozen
Waiting for a pin to drop
Weightless, aimless, deciding
It's not yet time to stop

I'm so fucking bored
But maybe bored isn't the right term
I've lost my motivation
And I don't know that I can find it again

I trace loose letters on white sheets
I don't see the words forming

Sensory Overload

My fingers twitch
My mind is on the brink
Of collapsing in on itself
My mouth is dry
My eyes are blank
Taking everything in
But not processing

I lie on rumpled sheets
Staring up at the ceiling
Feeling puffs of air escape my lips
And quiet energy in my fingertips
I close my eyes to shut it out
Sounds and smells come to a stop
My mind begins to race

I'm too awake to fall asleep
But still too numb to feel alive

Rut

Monotonously does each day pass
Each day more daunting than the last
So rare and few are the times between
That I glimpse a hint of things unseen

When I do it sparks a fire
Like water to an unclothed wire
Setting my bones aflame with light
Allowing my mind to take its flight

I wish those times came often but
The truth is too often I'm in a rut
I try to concede that it's not so vile
To be inspired only once in a while

Still I admire the people who
Always have thought for something new
Who find ideas in the oddest places
And create in ways that deserve graces

Because too often do I stare at the sky
Praying for something and asking why
I can't come up with something more
Than output others have seen before

Some may say I'm too hard on myself
But I feel like my mind's been on a shelf
And I wonder if it was better while
My mood was much more volatile

Not that I'd ever want to return
To the time when all would crash and burn
With a sideways glance, or slip of tongue
When my ladder was missing every rung

But there is, I think, some irony
In the thought that I had more creativity
When my mind was a riotous mess
And now that I am more, well, I have less

It's odd to think that pain's a trigger
Of thoughts so fierce and words so bitter
But it is and I can't change the fact
That the work I made, it has impact

What I make now seems to be amiss
Of the ferocity I had when I started this
I've tried to do the things I should
So why do I always feel it's not as good?

I don't think I'll ever stop what I'm doing
But I guess I'll have to start contending
With the fact that inspiration comes and goes
And sometimes highs just come with lows

But even then, I'll try my best
That when inspiration calls, I won't rest
'Cause after all that's all that I can do
That, and hope for something new

Maybe someday I'll find the spark again
Hold it close just like a friend
Ignite the flame like a luminary
And make of it something extraordinary

In the Rain

When the world lacks inspiration
And the days just pass you by
When nothing seems to matter
And yet your eyes are dry

It's not quite heavy sadness
But there's a weight in all your limbs
It's not a lack of purpose
But no smiles grace your lips

You lie in bed just waiting
For something to feel right to you
Wondering in the meanwhile
If it does, what will you do?

The sad truth is it could be there
Wanting you to take the reins
But with the way you're feeling
It's like there's ice in all your veins

And it's keeping you from moving
From doing something right
Your brain says, "Let's do something,"
Your body says, "Not tonight."

And somehow all the memories
They seem to be closing in
It's a never-ending cycle
It's a race you just can't win

And sometimes you might ask yourself
"Is this all there will ever be?
If this is what life has to offer,
Then what's the point of me?"

But dear, it's just depression,
Sad to say it, but it's true
And it's a bitter pill to swallow
When darkness has a hold on you

Oh, dear, it's just depression,
And someday dawn will break
Even if the pain is permanent
One day you'll weather the ache

And dear, it's just depression
It's a sickness with a name
In times when you feel like a pawn
Remember that you own the game

It's okay to lay down weapons,
It's okay to rest your soul
You've gotten through the worst of it
Did you think that that was all?

Did you think your wounds would disappear,
Without them leaving scars?
Did you think it would be easy to move on
After all you've done so far?

Allow the pain to settle
Allow the hurt to ache
Trust me when I tell you
Your heart's too strong to break

And one day when the dawn comes
Shining through your window pane,
You'll find that it was worth it,
All your time spent in the rain

One day when you smile again
You'll find purpose in all this
You'll discover who you've now become
And say goodbye to the child you'll miss

You'll find in you a strength so pure
And hold your head up high
Only then will you truly know
You've bid the dark goodbye

But until then, dear, it's okay
To nurse bruises from your fall
It's something we go through, all of us
We're human after all

Metaphors

I think it's only fitting that I write about writing, given how much I love doing it.

Words I weave on a shattered loom
They tangle in the threads of mutterings
Shadows dance in my living room
Rain seeps through tattered awnings

A broken seam begins to fray
Blank canvases stare judgmentally
A tired smile to my face makes way
For all moods go eventually

I reach for nothing but to see fingers grasp
At strands of nonexistent threads
Fingers curl like words around a gasp
And swirl like thoughts inside my head

A cacophony of sounds plays in my ears
I sink into the abyss of song
It's these same tunes that wore through tears
They now make me dance along

The night is quiet but for the sound
Of electricity humming in power lines
Similar to the energy I feel surrounds
Me on these melancholic times

Don't make a mistake about how I feel
I'm not as broken as I used to be
It's a little bit like I lost a wheel
And I'm learning to roll on tires of three

Most days are fine, though lacking cheer
But I've long since learned to let that go
There's more to life than joy so sheer
Fingers to the loom, I begin to sew

Yet sometimes I do feel the need
To stop and set my fabric down
When my thoughts, to despair they lead
Like plights upon unsuspecting towns

On times like those, I pray for words
To consume me with their warm embrace
It's not too long before I find the worlds
That take me back to my happy place

Meanings into words do I imbibe
Making use of metaphor or simile
For some things I can not describe
Except through verse and analogy

Stairwell

This poem is dedicated to a friend, who will hopefully never know it's about them.

Too often the lives we lead
Leave us in unexpected places
You were my friend when time began

Too often time is not enough
To move on, but that's what we do
Fake smiles cover what lies beneath

Am I the only one still hurting?
Do I need you to ease my pain?
Is it humility or madness,
That I just want to talk to you?

Should I just let it go?
Am I the only one still holding on?
Where's the real strength here?

It took me long to realize
That in the end, you helped me too
I don't even know if I'm convinced yet

Maybe I can let the relationship die
But how can a relationship like ours die?
My eyes are guarded every time I see you

Betrayal is betrayal, isn't it?
Then why do I keep giving you a chance?
Nothing was ever final with me

I cry to you in a stairwell,
Hug you tight when you call my name
But in the back of my mind, I hear
The deafening silence once again

And I just don't know what to do
Who even are you to me anymore?
I guess I'll never know

My pain has made me stronger
That much I know for sure
But have you?

I guess thinking of you will always lead
To unanswered questions
And this poem will never be finished

Better Times

At least for me, depression hasn't been a constant state of sadness. There were times I felt alive and still had depression. There were times I felt the most loved despite feeling hopeless. There were times I was filled with so much joy it felt like I could explode from every inch of my body with cheer.
"Better Times" talks about all those moments, and the ones to come.

Here's to the feeling of blood in our veins
Here's to the nights when we felt awake
Here's to the beds we left empty and cold
Here's to the streets that we walked alone

Here's to the sounds we heard in surround
Here's to the moods we tried to write down
Here's to the world in technicolor
Here's to the days we couldn't ask for more

There were moments when all tears were spent
There were times when words filled up a breath
There were days when the past seemed so far away
There were nights when the joy didn't want to wait

There was magic in the air that came alive upon waking
There was life in the soil that was ripe for the taking
There was a face in the crowd with the softest smile
There was solitude and solace to be found in the meanwhile

Here's to the dreams we dreamt wide awake
Here's to the chances we decided we'd take
Here's to the people we forgave and forgot
Here's to the sins we didn't give a thought

Here's to anticipation and here's to song
Here's to all the people whom we brought along
Here's to the moments our cheeks were all dry
Here's to the better times we can't ever deny

There's a world that is waiting for those times to return
There's a mood that is ailing to crash and to burn
There's a life that is gaining momentum to be born
There's a light beyond the tunnel and peace after the storm

There's life to be had in the space out there
There's peace to be found in this world somewhere
There's joy to be savored, and love to be flavored
And one day we'll wake, and shake off this nightmare

When before becomes after and future becomes past
Those better times will come back, and make their home at last

A Little Hint of Hoping

I wrote "A Little Hint of Hoping" while commuting home one night. I had just seen an announcement from the University for a writing competition, and on the bus ride all I could think was that joining the competition meant giving myself a chance to want something again, after such a long time of living in hopelessness.
I didn't win the competition, but I do think I won something far greater.

A little hint of hoping
Dare I try to make believe?
Can I forget the tide that's ever-flowing
And indulge in some relief?

A touch of wishful thinking
A bolt from the figurative blue
A show of shaky confidence
And defiance to rejection, too

Dare I hope and dare I dream?
The future was never so bright before
Crystalline and sparkling
Leaving me wanting more

Both a destination and a pit stop
On life's long and winding road
It could be a silver lining
Or it could be another load

On shoulders already heavy
With burdens hard to bear
So with every breath I ask myself,
Do I stay, or do I dare?

It's not quite light at the end of the tunnel
But a crack in the concrete
It's not a finished product
But a blot of ink upon a sheet

A spotlight waiting on a stage
For its performer to sing a song
That'll spear hearts through with melody
And make lips dance along

So many second chances
Have long since passed me by
Do I let this one go,
Or do I jump in and try?

A golden opportunity
Is the term that they would use
But chances are choices first and foremost
And it's time for me to choose

It doesn't have a simple answer
If I were someone else, it might
But just because I am myself
Does that mean I've lost the fight?

There's no conclusion to this story
My choice remains unmade
But that's not always a problem
Because the little hope's remained

And maybe it's enough
To have a little hope laid bare
Because hope's a feisty, stubborn thing
And after all, we all start somewhere

Muse

> Where would I be without the people who helped me
> get where I am?

It must have hurt to see me cry
And know you couldn't help
It must have felt so powerless
Knowing my problem was myself

When I didn't laugh at any jokes
And stared blankly at the wall
It must have pained to see me so numb
And wonder how far I would fall

In my darkest times I wonder why
You dared to stick around
I searched long and hard for reasons but
In the end love's what I found

You were the lighthouse that I sought
After years in a stormy sea
You taught me what commitment was
By never giving up on me

You taught me there can be relief
In bringing myself to try
You taught me that if I dare to ask
Help is never in short supply

You trusted me to find my way
Even when trees blocked my path
When I lost faith in who I was
You knew I'd recover in the aftermath

It's your constant faith that brought me here
Your belief that made me strong
Even if I didn't know my place
I know where I'll always belong

And even though you have your faults
I learned to forgive them in order to grow
I may not always say it, but
You've done more for me than you'll ever know

In daytime you're my sanctuary
In darkness, my candle light
You're the setting of every story I tell,
The muse of every poem I write

You're so integral to who I am
So I wish there was more I could do
But I guess I'll settle for loving you back
And dedicating this poem to you

If I tried to say all that I mean
This poem would have no end
So instead I'll make it short and sweet:
You are my closest friends

Just know that I'll be grateful for
The rest of my life for you
And I'll be keeping you in my heart
Until my days are through

Mocha

I will forever be grateful for and to the people who supported me, but I would be amiss if I didn't talk about how my pets helped me survive depression.
Mocha was a rabbit, my first pet, and more comfort to me than I'd ever thought an animal could be.

Thank you for your silence
That was calm and comforting
Thank you for your presence
On which I was relying
Thank you for your audience
On the times that I was blue
Thank you that my burdens
Left me when I cuddled you

Thank you for the part of me
Eight years with you has made
Thank you for all you taught me
And everything you gave
Thank you for trusting me
And for being my best try
Thank you for loving me back
Thank you always, and goodbye

Whiskey

One day, a stray cat snuck into our house to give birth. We put the kittens in a box with blankets for her to pick up, and she took them all with her but one—the one who, I suppose, was the runt of the litter. This was a particularly bad time in my life, and the last thing I expected was for a blessing to come to me in the form of a cat. I'd never even wanted a cat before. But I took one look at that tiny thing, so fragile and dependent and needy, and I couldn't turn away. Unfortunately, the precious animal only survived for a couple of days. Before I could even give it a name, my new pet was gone. And I was ready to throw myself into another bout of depression, but I had already made a promise to the cat—a promise to take care of myself so I could take care of it.

This poem is for Whiskey, the pet I never had.

I always wondered what your eyes would look like
You had the softest fur I ever felt
I'd feel your tiny limbs push my palms when you weren't even there

I'm so sorry you only got a name when you were gone
I'm sorry I never knew if you were a boy or a girl
I'm sorry I couldn't get to know you

They told me never be too happy
Or something's bound to go wrong
I'm so sorry I was laughing without knowing you'd died

I wanted to show you off to my friends
Say, "This. This is mine. I love this."
I guess I'll save that for next time

I wanted you to be Whiskey and the gentlest girl
You would prove to me that it wasn't a paradox
That an unbreakable spirit can match the softest heart

If people would scoff I wouldn't care
Say, "Cats are aloof and they don't love you,"
I would know better

Because I saw it in your eyes
I saw your complete trust in me
And I felt the fear in my heart that told me it was love

Someday I'll be asked if I ever had a cat
And I'll say that I did
Because I don't care if it was only two days

You were my cat and I loved you
You were my cat and I miss you still

You came at a time when I needed you most
And I thought you were here to stay
But I guess only the memory is

I had so many dreams for you
You were gonna be my closest friend
Now our friendship is buried with you

But I promised you, didn't I?
I said it on your grave
I told you I'll keep going

So keep going I will
Because even when you're gone
Your lesson should be unforgettable

And keep going I will
Because you gave me the strength to
When I was falling apart

You came to me
And you made me care about you
So keep going I will

I hope I really did do you right
I hope what I did made passing a little easier
And I hope you're happy now

I love you, okay?
I can now say I've fallen in love at first sight
Because I saw you and the darkness went away

And it'll come back but
Right now that's okay
Because from you I learned

Keep going, I will.

Lucky, Pt. 1

After the events that inspired "Whiskey," I was gifted with another two blessings—a Siamese cat named Perry, and a Persian cat named Lucky. Lucky was a gift from my neighbor, whose cats had recently had a litter and who were giving away or selling their older cats. I got Lucky at no cost, though I would soon discover how priceless he truly was.

Lucky was almost doglike in the way he followed us around, doted on us, and brightened up our days. He loved every single member of my family, even my brother who was averse to most animals. According to my neighbor, he had been ill as a kitten, and almost didn't make it. That was hard to believe with how healthy he seemed. After a year, however, Lucky passed from kidney failure. When I lost him, it was so sudden that I never got to say goodbye. It still hurts to think about him. But I try to remember how happy he made us, and that's enough to keep me moving on.

Baby, will I see you in heaven?
No one deserves it more than you
Can you see me from heaven,
After all that we've been through?

Will you be there in heaven,
Waiting to run into my arms?
Are you up there now in heaven,
Watching from afar?

Baby, what's it like in heaven?
Should I trust that you're now okay?
'Cause loving you was so easy
And losing you hurt more than I can say

Is your pain gone now in heaven?
Can that be my consolation prize?
Are you up with God in heaven,
Seeing Him with your golden eyes?

Do you know that He took care of you,
Kept you strong so we could meet?
He must have known how much I needed you,
Now you're gone it's like I can't breathe

And I'll keep moving on without you
Or at least I'll try my best
Without the weight of you within my arms,
Ignoring the missing piece in my chest

What if I don't see you in heaven?
What if I never get to say goodbye?
Will you ever know how I truly felt,
The first day you made me cry?

I only had you for a year
And it will never be enough
If I never see you in heaven,
And never thank you for your love

So I'll pray to the God who made you
And blessed me with you way back then
That at least for just one moment
He'll let me see you once again

And I'll wait to go to heaven
Till the day we meet once more
If I see you in heaven
It'll be all that I've wished for

And if one day in heaven
You see me coming through
I hope you'll be there waiting
'Cause I'll be waiting for you, too

Lucky, Pt. 2

If cats could smile, you would have
Because you were one of a kind
If cats could hug, you would have
Because we were always on your mind

You couldn't praise but you would have,
Had you been blessed with words
You couldn't laugh but you would have,
To you, everything was right in the world

Instead of smiles you gave us meowing,
Of the loud yet precious kind,
You couldn't hug but you would cuddle,
The most affectionate cat I'd ever find

And even though you still were cat-like
You taught me that cats could be
The sweetest creatures in the world
Who show love so innocently

I called you baby because that's who you were,
So childlike in your joy
So accepting of anyone, no matter who
My only baby boy

If I'd known you were going, I would have
Been there to hold you close
So many things I'd do if I'd been there
My regret for that only grows

And until now it makes me sad
That I couldn't say goodbye
I can't finish the sentence, "If you were here . . . "
Because if you were, I'd never cry

It hurts to say "I loved you,"
Because it feels like moving on
So instead I'll say the next best thing:
To me, you were inspiration

You inspired me to laugh a lot,
To face each day with a smile
To show a love that's limitless
To appreciate the meanwhile

You inspired me to take it slow
To take all that life will give
To show affection in all ways that I can
And most of all, to live

Because in the year that you were with us,
You were the happiest cat I'd ever seen
You made it hard to say goodbye
To the cat you could have been

So now I'll tell myself instead
Maybe Someone Up There needs your smile
Because I know no matter where you are
You'll be making life worthwhile

So I'll keep you in my memory
Remember you as my friend
And stay inspired by who you were
Until I see you once again

An Open Letter to My Heart

I've been through a lot. If you're anything like me, then you've probably been through a lot, too. But there's something to be said about us: we're still here, and we're still fighting.

Here's an open letter to my heart
And all that it's been through:
There's a precious kind of love I feel
Every time I think of you

You started off so full of peace
Secure in all that was,
Flesh and blood and beating love,
A wall of unbroken glass

And even when the struggles came
You never stopped your song
You dreamt of hope and fantasy
Even with no one to sing along

When came the time for your first crack
You didn't know what to do
It hurts to think that loneliness
Made itself a home in you

And as the crack grew bigger
You tried to fill it with concrete,
Prioritizing others over yourself
And idolizing everyone you meet

In time you learned to harden
But never quite realized
You were encased in stone, but even so
You were soft and sad inside

And one day the glass shattered
All your shells, they broke apart
And you saw the truth for what it was:
You were a broken heart

And oh, you thought that was the end
You couldn't see the light
And yet you beat for all you had
Without an end in sight

Because to beat was all you knew
To keep going every single day
Even when the end was out of your reach,
Somehow you found your way

And one day when the morning came
You faced your fears once more
You built new walls of wood and cloth,
And this time built a door

You got the help you needed and
Forgave to ease your pain
Little by little, you began to find
The sun after all the rain

And now you're back to normal
If a little worse for wear
And I'm stronger than I've ever been
Thanks to your loving care

To end this letter to my heart,
I think all I can say
Is I'll do my best to stay true to love
And love myself everyday

If there's one thing you've taught me
Something I keep thinking of
It's that I should be here for a cause
And what better cause than love?

Soulmate

I always thought I couldn't write a romantic poem because I'd never had a romantic relationship. Thus, "Soulmate" was quite the surprise.

I don't know what your name is
I don't know what you'll make of this
But I hope it soothes your mind

Knowing that you don't wait alone
'Cause just like you I've always known
That there was someone for me to find

I don't know where you're coming from
Or if, like me, your heart is numb
But someday I know we'll meet

And crash like waves upon a shore
Dance along a kitchen floor
Move to a shared heartbeat

If I could find you now, I would
Hold you close just like I should
But I guess that'll have to wait

So darling, just hold tight and pray
'Cause you and I will meet someday
And in God's time, no one is late

There are days when I feel insecure
There are days when I think I'm not sure
That I can love like you'll need me to

'Cause I'm not the easiest to love
I have many flaws I can think of
I'm sorry, dear, what can I do?

But there are days when I know better
I know you can't be perfect either
And if I'll accept; then why won't you?

So when you're lonely, trust I understand
I wish that I could hold your hand
But for now this is all we can be

Time can be an unforgiving teacher
If I could reach into my future
I swear I'd bring you home to me

But one day our stars, they will align
So I'll wait for the day I see your smile
And have your voice sing me to sleep

And until then, I'll wait for you
Time is ours when this game is through
And every promise to you I'll keep

So listen, dear, don't be distraught
Our waiting game is not for naught
Our lives are still in tune

And if time is all that it takes
I swear I'd wait a thousand days
If it means I'll meet you soon

Clapback

I've met so many people who were beneficial to my growth, but as with anyone else, there have also been people who tried to put me down. I've learned, however, that loving myself and owning who I am are far more powerful than any rebuttal I could make. So, here's a poem to celebrate that.

Call me your names
They'll fall on deaf ears
Play all the games
I've been playing for years

Destroy me with words
They'll fall at my feet
Would you still be this cruel,
If you and I were to meet?

Slouch behind your screen
And start typing away
You don't have what it takes
To take me on today

I'm high on a cloud
Your sentiments can't reach
I'm deep in a feeling
Your little words can't preach

I've spent far too long
Fortifying my walls
It'll take more than your comments
For them to crumble and fall

I've hated myself too
Long to let your words shatter
I've grown to love myself too
Much for your thoughts to matter

And if you knew better
You'd be silent, too
Knowing your words
Are more reflective of you

How can you hurt me?
You don't know what I've been through
You don't even know me,
Trust me, I have more complaints than you

I've seen flaws and limitations
But also the heart that lies beneath
I've learned to accept them
And found myself underneath

I could be like you
For we both know my faults
But I'm not like you
For I love me despite them all

And if you were like me
Maybe you'd give the world a chance
And learn to look beyond
What you see at first glance

Maybe you'd be nicer
To people who are just like you
Maybe you'd be understanding
Of what we all go through

And maybe you'd be happier
Putting your own self in your place
And maybe you'd feel better
After you've changed your ways

So I wish you good luck
Watch you let your hatred out
'Cause we both know it's not me
You really feel bad about

And I'll be there for you
When the tables have turned
'Cause we also know it's not me
Who's the one getting burned

By the words that you spit
Like they're fire on your tongue
There might have been a time when
Those words might have stung

But trust me when I say this:
You're hurting you more than me
And when you learn to love yourself,
You'll understand what I see

So I hope you learn to love yourself,
And that it teaches you to be kind
Until then, if you want to hate on me
Trust that I won't even mind

The Body I Bear

I used to hate my body so much, and to be honest, I'm still struggling to feel good about it. But this poem seems like a step in the right direction.

I put so much thought
Into the clothes that I wear
Without ever prioritizing
The body that I bear

I give so much importance
To the mind that I hone
Without any consideration
For the body that I own

My moods and thoughts run rampant,
As my soul I appreciate,
But what's a soul without its shell,
The body that I understate?

I take you for granted all the time
Despite all that you've been through
I don't always consider that
There wouldn't be a "me" without you

There are even times I hate you
When expectations start kicking in
And the world's standards weigh me down
And I feel like I just can't win

But your hands write what I see in my head
And your feet take me to places
Your eyes see the world for what it can be
And your weight fills in the spaces

Your lungs take in the precious air
That keeps me alive and awake
Your limbs hold close the ones I love
And create all I want to make

Most of all your beating heart
Pumps life into my veins
Of the life I've been blessed to have and lead,
You've given me all the reins

And I can't even promise that
I'll always see your worth
Just know that I am happy that
You're the one I've had since birth

'Cause you've been able to live through
So much life's thrown your way
Would it be corny of me to say that
Without you, I wouldn't be where I am today?

So this here is my ode to you
'Cause really, it's unfair
That I keep forgetting all about
The body that I bear

And this here is my poem for you
Big or small, fat or thin
It doesn't matter 'cause now I love
The body that I'm in

And as this poem comes to a close
To conclude all that's above:
I'll try my best, to call you now
The body that I love

Youth, Pt. 1

And now, my dear readers, I dedicate these last couple of poems to you.

When the world goes dark
And even mornings are gray
When there's no sunlight

When the hurt makes a home
Of your body and soul
When the voices are endless

When the world seems so cruel
When comfort isn't enough
And everything starts to change

Every hour brings an ache
You're just barely moving
And it's not because you want to

I won't claim to understand
All that you're going through
But know that you're not alone

I know you don't know me
I'm just a face in the crowd
But like a prayer

I'm sending out a plea
To the universe for you
And I pray the universe listens

I was once where you are now
And there are days when I go back
To my own darkest niches

And all that I can say to you
Is that if you reach out a hand
I'll be reaching back

Because all we can do
In this world full of fear
Is find someone who'll ease the pain

And maybe you don't know it yet
But you've got me in your corner
Cheering you on from this side of the world

And maybe you don't see it yet
But one day it'll get better
Because nothing lasts forever

And the world waits for you
To rise up and claim your place
And I'll be watching you smile

As you take hold of your prize
And finally know
You're where you need to be

Youth, Pt. 2

Got so much light inside you
Yet you sit there in the dark
You're waiting for a fire to start
Don't you know that you're the spark?

Your self-restraint is running thin
As you wait to see the sun
Keeping yourself down on your knees
Ready to get up and run

Hey, you
The world doesn't know it yet
But it needs you in it
So ready, set—

Go where your blood keeps pounding
Go where your heart's alive
Go where your mind wanders
Go where your love can thrive

You've spent so long in darkness
That you forgot your own heart light
You've been held back for far too long
You've forgotten how to fight

You may not know who I am
In the crowd, I'm just a face
But know that I have utter faith
That in this world, you'll find your place

Hey, you
There's no need to regret
But you can change
So ready, set—

Go where your light will shine so bright
Go where your heart opens
Go where you can be a beacon of hope
Go where you'll make a difference

Don't be afraid to leave behind
The ones that choose to stay
Forge your path and make your mark
For what matters never goes away

And the world had better be prepared
'Cause you're going to make it through
Whoever you are, whatever you've done
You're gonna remake the world anew

Hey, you
No need to be upset
It's your time now
So ready, set—

Go where life is calling
Go where time stands still
Go where joy's abundant
Go and have your fill

Go and just remember
The child you used to be
It's your turn now to pave the way
For others to be free

www.ingramcontent.com/pod-product-compliance
Lightning Source LLC
LaVergne TN
LVHW051704080426
835511LV00017B/2726